MW00774098

CRANIAL CONSTIPATION

CRANIAL CONSTIPATION

Proven Ways to Let Go of
Sh!tty Thoughts and Cr@ppy Ideas

Rusty Williams

The Barefoot Ministries

CRANIAL CONSTIPATION

Proven Ways to Let Go of Sh!tty Thoughts and Cr@ppy Ideas

Copyright © 2023 by Rusty Williams.

ISBN: 979-8-9886245-2-3 (paperback edition)

ISBN: 978-1-7361579-9-2 (eBook edition)

First printing edition 2023

Published by The Barefoot Ministries

Medford Lakes, NJ 08055

www.thebarefootministries.org

This book is dedicated to anyone who has ever been accused of having *shit for brains*.

"Let go or be dragged."

~ Zen proverb

Table of Contents

Strategy #1: Take a breather and take notice of the world around you. Strategy #2: Compare your thoughts to what you are experiencing. Strategy #3: Distance yourself from your thoughts. Strategy #4: Choose where you focus your attention. Strategy #5: Remind yourself that it's normal to have negative thoughts.

Strategy #6: Identify what makes the thought you're having a bad thought. Strategy #7: Breathe! Strategy #8: Grab a coloring book and some colored pencils. Strategy #9: Listen to calming music. Strategy #10: Change the energy by changing your location.

Strategy #11: Take a walk. Strategy #12: Get some exercise (*after consulting your doctor). Strategy #13: Question yourself if there is evidence to support your thought. Strategy #14: Will it matter a year from now? Five years from now? Strategy #15: Give mindfulness, or another form of meditation, a try.

Strategy #16: Put your thoughts in perspective without judging them. Strategy #17: Remember a time when you moved on without any real damage. Strategy #18: Cook or bake. Strategy #19: Re-read your favorite feel-good book. Strategy #20: Take in a game or show.

Strategy #21: Find those old photos from your past that bring back good memories. Strategy #22: Practice letting go of what doesn't serve you well. Strategy #23: Challenge the idea that you have to control everything in order to be content. Strategy #24: Write it down and then get rid of it. Strategy #25: Talk to a trusted friend or loved one.

Strategy #26: Call a counselor or therapist (or a crisis hotline). Strategy #27: Practice positive affirmations. Strategy #28: Make a mental list of your positive attributes. Strategy #29: Remind yourself that it's okay to not be okay. Strategy #30: Recognize what triggers negative thoughts.

Strategy #31: Make a list of your success (wins) for the week. Strategy #32: Step out of your comfort zone and do something different. Strategy #33: Do random acts of kindness. Strategy #34: Smile. Strategy #35: Change your body position.

Strategy #36: Commit to making one healthy food choice that day. Strategy #37: Laugh! Strategy #38: Yell into your head, "Stop!" Strategy #39: Practice gratitude. Strategy #40: Set a time limit for any unproductive thoughts.

Strategy #41: Create a positive and fun anchor. Strategy #42: Stop any comparison to others in similar situations. Strategy #43: Stop "should have" self-talk. Strategy #44: Recognize automatic negative thoughts. Strategy #45: Identity what kind of emotions are attached to negative thoughts.

Strategy #46: Embrace the thought and sit with it for a minute. Strategy #47: Chunk the problem down to manageable things you can tackle. Strategy #48: Build or create something in your mind. Strategy #49: Go on a virtual shopping spree. Strategy #50: Enjoy a soothing cup of tea or hot cocoa.

Strategy #51: Practice reframing the situation. Strategy #52: Practice self-acceptance. Strategy #53: Teach something to someone. Strategy #54: Tell someone why you appreciate them. Strategy #55: What advice would you give a friend if they were having the same thoughts?

Strategy #56: Convert your inner critic into your inner cheerleader. Strategy #57: Accept your shortcomings. Strategy #58: Stop second-guessing yourself. Strategy #59: Think about what's possible. Strategy #60: The worst possible thing isn't going to happen!

Strategy #61: Develop an attitude of gratitude. Strategy #62: Create new neuropathways by creating new habits. Strategy #63: Limit editorial news and media. Strategy #64: Create a safe place in your mind. Strategy #65: You're not a mind-reader.

Introduction

Some thoughts to consider as you begin this book.

What do you do with a turd?

Seriously, what do you do with a turd?

Ok, let's ask it a different way: What *should* you do with a turd?

Are you still wondering why you're being asked to consider this? Especially at the very beginning of a book? Welcome to the world of *Cranial Constipation*!

Maybe if it's posed in a more thoughtful way, would that help?

Here goes: What is the *healthiest* thing to do with a turd?

It's unlikely anyone would disagree that the healthiest thing to do with a turd is to get rid of it. It's universally accepted as this is not just the healthiest thing to do with a turd, but it's also what should be done with it. And I'm willing to bet it's what you do with it—every day.

Every day, a certain amount of time in our lives is spent getting rid of turds.

If we don't get rid of a turd, what happens to us?

One turd turns into two turds, and then they turn into a few more until our entire system gets backed up. The medical professions (and more than a few drug companies) have a name for this kind of backup. They call it *constipation*.

Other than if there is nowhere to leave it, none of us would purposely hold onto a turd. While small children have been known to refuse to let go of a turd, adults don't purposely hold on to them. In fact, as we age, most adults look for different ways (and medications) to make sure the turds in our lives are let go of without much effort. We adults will do anything we can to avoid becoming constipated; we know all too well the pain and discomfort that comes with clogged bowels.

I would submit to you one more adult truth: We also know the pain and discomfort that comes when we hold onto sh!tty thoughts and cr@ppy ideas. We know the mental anguish, the fear and anxiety, and even the physical ache caused when we can't (or won't) let go of these thoughts. And yet, for reasons that are paradoxically personal to each of us and universally similar, we believe that by holding onto them, we are accomplishing something that might eventually make us feel better.

And while it's well beyond the scope of this book to discuss the hows and whys people hold onto unhealthy thoughts, it is well within the scope of practice of the author to offer suggestions on how to easily let go of them and move forward in life. I say that because I know the author and he's a decent guy (most of the time). I should know him very well . . . the author is me. And you, the reader, have a right to know a little bit about me, the author, if you're going to accept anything I say as beneficial to you in this journey we call life.

So, here goes. My post-graduate degrees are in pastoral counseling and ministry; I was ordained into the Christian Church in 2008. At that time, I was serving with a police department in southern New Jersey as a detective, and I retired from that department after 25 years of service in 2010. During those couple of years when I was both an ordained minister and a detective, I'm happy to share with you that I never once confused last rites with Miranda rights!

Prior to becoming a police officer, I was a paramedic for five years. In the thirty years I was involved in emergency services, I was exposed to countless situations that caused sh!tty thoughts and cr@ppy ideas. It would be more than five years after I retired before I learned the importance of letting go of them, and some of the methods I used will be shared in the pages you are about to read.

As a minister, I've sat and listened to people from all walks of life with a variety of life's problems. A common thread in our discussions was the thoughts consuming their minds as they tried to figure out a plan of action that would get them on a path they envisioned for themselves.

I'm also a police chaplain, serving the police department in the town where my wife, Elissa, and I live. In this role, I'm asked to intervene in any number of situations, some of which are sh!tty thoughts and cr@ppy ideas that lead to circumstances that cause my cell phone to ring.

Because of a tumor growing in my spinal cord, I am in constant (chronic) pain. As you might imagine, living with constant pain can lead to sh!tty thoughts and cr@ppy ideas. And, if not for the insistence by my wife to seek an alternative way of dealing with it, it's doubtful this book (or any of my books) would have been written.

Elissa all but dragged me to see a hypnotist where I would learn to control my pain, *Yeah, right!* I was an ordained minister and a retired police detective; there was no way I could ever be hypnotized. That's what I told Elissa. What ended up happening was that it helped me so much that I became a hypnotist myself, specializing in medical hypnosis, and I'm also a hypnosis instructor.

Finally, I am also a facilitator for resiliency training for first responders. In that role, I share some of my past traumas and successes and discuss strategies that help develop and strengthen a resilient mindset. Many of the tips offered in this book are also shared with the participants in resiliency training workshops.

So now what do you think? Maybe there are a few tricks up my sleeve, and if there are, I'm grateful to be able to share them with anyone who will listen. Why? Because I spent too many years doing it wrong—holding onto unhealthy thoughts and bad ideas, thinking that by doing so, I was accomplishing something positive. The pain I caused myself (by holding onto them) was unnecessary, and it is truly only by dumb luck and the love of family and friends that I was able to come through all the storms in my life with a new outlook and an attitude of gratitude.

Before going any further, there's one thing I must ask of you: Do not think of a white bear.

That's all there is to it; just don't think of a white bear.

Where was I? An attitude of gratitude.

If there is one goal of mine with this book, it's this: I sincerely hope that the tips and strategies in this book will help you develop an attitude where you search for reasons to be grateful.

4

Life is too short to not fully understand the strength of being grateful and the health benefits that come from it.

With that idea of gratitude as a theme, what do you say that we get moving with the tips and strategies?

But first, without belaboring the point, why in living hell would anyone intentionally hold onto a turd?

Makes you think, doesn't it?

If gratitude is the theme of this book, then a white bear is the foundation for everything you'll read from this point forward.

You remember, don't you? Just don't think of a white bear.

It sounds easy, doesn't it? It sounds easy, but in reality, your brain is doing some behind-the-scenes work that is reinforcing an image of a white bear. Even though you are doing your best to not think about it, your brain is creating an image of it—just to make sure you aren't thinking about it.

Let me explain.

Suppressing the White Bear

As with everything shared in this book, the idea of trying to forget a white bear is based on research. Yes, all the tips and strategies in the pages that follow are based on proven methods with foundations based on sound research and peer-reviewed studies. Hey, the subtitle might be sh!tty and cr@ppy, but the content of this book is filled with proven methods (the other part of the subtitle) that have helped people from all walks of life—just like you—let go of thoughts and ideas that no longer served them well.

When you were asked not to think of a white bear, what did you first have to do? More specifically, what did your brain first have to do? Your brain had to first identify what it was that you were asked *not* to think about. For you to understand what it was that you *weren't* supposed to do, your brain had to search for an image of that (somewhere in your memory) so it knew what it *wasn't* supposed to do. In other words, it is impossible to not think of something without first thinking of it.

This idea of not being able to not think about something without thinking about it (yeah, good luck following that train of thought) was first written about by the Russian author Fyodor

Dostoyevsky in 1863. Dostoyevsky wrote about his travels and asked the reader: *"Try to pose for yourself this task: not to think of a polar bear, and you will see that the cursed thing will come to mind every minute."*

Fast-forward more than a century later, a psychology professor at Harvard named Dr. Daniel Wegner decided to look into this further. He referred to this as "suppressing the white bear" because he advised the participants in the research not to think of a white bear. Dr. Wegner discovered that there is, as he described it, a rebound effect where thoughts that are trying to be suppressed come back more prominently later. He theorized that as one part of the brain does what it needs to do to not think about something (in his studies, a white bear), another part of the brain continually checks in to ensure a white bear isn't being thought about. A feedback loop of sorts is created; the more (and harder) one tries not to think about something, the more another part of the brain checks in to ensure it's not thinking about it.

This is why it makes no sense to tell someone to "just not think about it." The same holds true when we, in trying to help, tell a friend or loved one not to worry about something or to not be afraid. The more they try not to think about it, the more the thought will reappear in their mind; the more they try not to worry or be afraid, the more their worry and fear will show up in their minds—and the stronger it will become.

This is why the findings of Dr. Wegner's research are the foundation for the tips and strategies in this book, as well as the admonition that holding onto a turd is ridiculous!

So, what do you say that we dive into the ways you can let go of that turd instead of trying to pretend it doesn't exist? Because ignoring that it's there or trying to not think about it, as research shows, will lead to cranial constipation. And nobody wants to walk around with a mind filled with sh!tty thoughts and cr@ppy ideas.

How to Use This Book

While there is no wrong way to use this book (other than, perhaps, as an adjustable shim to level an uneven leg on your coffee table or washing machine), there is more than one right way to read it.

For some, starting with the first tip and going chronologically from there will work best. For others, it might be looking at the table of contents and choosing a strategy that seems the best fit or the most comfortable to start. And, then there's the "we'll let fate decide" method; this is where you go to the table of contents, close your eyes, and point to a place on the page— wherever your finger lands, that's where you go, and you take it from there.

Whichever way you choose, it's best to practice that tip for about a week before moving on to the next one. This way, you'll be giving yourself the opportunity to be honest about your efforts . . . and your success. Yes, you will be successful in learning the best ways to let go of sh!tty thoughts and cr@ppy ideas! And, since there are 65 strategies, you'll have more than a year's worth of successes and wins, and you know that's going to make you feel good about yourself.

I bet you can already see yourself now as being free of that stuff and feeling how good it feels to let go of the mental turds that used to be clogging your mind (and perhaps your judgment). Hey, maybe you'll be feeling so good that people will be taking notice, and you will be discovered by a talent agent for a laxative commercial: See yourself smiling and dancing in some whimsical field or meadow while upbeat music is playing in the background as a voiceover actor says, "You too can feel this light and free!"

Okay, enough of the setup; it's time for you to start on the best day(s) of your life.

The Strategies

Leave who you were.
Love who you are.
Look forward to who you will become.
~ Unknown

Strategy #1

Take a breather and take notice of the world around you.

Taking a moment to simply pause and count to 30 distracts your mind to focus on something other than your thoughts. You're using a different area of your brain when you count than when you ruminate over a thought.

This is taken a step further when you take notice of everything around you. Where are you? What do you see in this place? What do you hear (even if it's your thoughts… or your own heartbeat)? What are you feeling, both mentally and physically? Can you feel whatever is on your feet? And, if you're barefoot, what does that feel like? What about what you're wearing—can you feel certain parts of your clothes against your skin? What about any smells or even tastes (in the event you're reading this part of the book while you're eating)?

This focusing on your surroundings is a simple way to practice mindfulness and mindfulness has been shown to be an effective way to let go of ruminating thoughts.

Practice this a couple of times a day and before you know it, you'll look forward to it throughout the week!

Strategy #2

Compare your thoughts to what you are experiencing.

This simple technique gives you the opportunity to be with your thoughts instead of attempting to ignore them. Really give your thoughts some thought (yeah, I know…), and then compare them to what you are experiencing at that moment. This is similar to Strategy #1 in that you'll focus on what you are experiencing—this time using your senses *and* your emotions.

Do you feel safe where you are at this very moment? Are you comfortable (is the temperature to your liking, is your body position strong, is your comfort level where it needs to be, etc.)? Are there reasons in your life to be happy or grateful (for anything)?

Practicing this will help train your brain to stop the "what if" trap and prime it to be in the present.

As with most things in life, the more you practice this, the better you feel, and the better you feel, the more you'll want to use it.

Strategy #3

Distance yourself from your thoughts.

This is a form of mindfulness; at least, it's a component. In mindfulness, the practitioner becomes aware of what they're experiencing from the perspective of an observer. Notice, again, that no one is suggesting that whatever is being experienced is to be ignored or not thought about. Instead, those thoughts are experienced from a different perspective—literally.

Rather than experiencing the thoughts from the first-person standpoint (as we have been doing all our lives), you shift your perspective (and mindset) and see them from a third-person point of view. From this unique vantage point, you will see these thoughts as just being there. When this is practiced, those thoughts lose their power and any control they once had in your life.

Once you've become comfortable with this, you can take it a step further. See those thoughts from the point of view of an observer—simply seeing them there, then shift the perspective again to a place where you are watching you (the observer) looking at those thoughts and notice how neutral they really are. Sure, some might call this a form of astral travel, but nothing in this book suggests you can't have fun with these strategies!

Strategy #4

Choose where you focus your attention.

Imagine you are in a dark room and the only light source you have is a flashlight. You can only see where you shine the light, and only whatever in the room is illuminated by that beam of light can be processed by your brain. The room is filled with all kinds of things, but you can only concentrate on whatever you are shining the light on.

The same is true with your thoughts. Whatever you shine a light on (wherever you focus your attention), those thoughts are what become processed by your brain. But what if you decided to shine your light around the room and see what else is there? You'd be giving yourself the opportunity to examine the other things in that room, wouldn't you?

You wouldn't be making believe that things in the room really weren't there (your thoughts); instead, you would simply be controlling where you aim that light—what you choose to focus on. You can do the same thing with your thoughts by focusing your attention on other—more positive—things in your life.

Strategy #5

Remind yourself that it's normal to have negative thoughts.

Another way to put this is to think of all the storms in life that you've survived so far. Your success rate is 100 percent. It has to be . . . otherwise, you wouldn't be reading this right now!

As "cliché-ish" as this might sound, you are a survivor; you've survived every storm you've encountered. So there's no reason to think you won't survive this one. Those past storms have given you every reason to believe you are a winner. You've won each one of those contests.

Now you can look back and use that proven track record to see how, as you collect win after win, you are strong and will add one more check mark to the win column!

Hey, you've made it through all the previous bad thoughts, so there's no reason to think you won't make it through others.

Strategy #6

Identify what makes the thought you're having a bad thought.

Something I've learned dealing with a chronic illness is that pain doesn't become suffering until we attach an emotion to it. And that is what I share with hypnosis clients who come to see me for pain control. If the statement about suffering is true for pain and emotions, isn't it also true for thoughts and feelings?

If you think about something that causes you difficulty, it's all but impossible not to attach an emotion to it. So, rather than trying to convince yourself that you're not feeling something or that the emotion doesn't exist, you can examine the emotion separately from the thought.

Additionally, when the thinking part of the brain is used to figure out a problem, the emotional part of it can take a short break.

So, by taking some time to consider what (in your mind) makes the thought a bad thought, you're training your brain to develop new thought pathways that use problem-solving instead of going back to your emotions.

Strategy #7

Breathe!

Think about this: How often are you consciously aware of your breathing? Breathing is something we do every day, all day long—awake and sleeping. And maybe because we do it so often, we don't really think about it. But when we focus on the breath, we shift our attention away from other thoughts.

One of the best ways to intentionally breathe is to practice what is called "box breathing." Box breathing is breathing in four distinct stages and those stages are equal in time. Those stages are inhalation, hold, exhalation, and pause. Each stage is like a side of a box.

It works like this:

- Breathe in for four seconds—count to yourself, one-thousand one, one-thousand two, one-thousand three, one-thousand four.

- Hold that breath for four seconds.

- Exhale slowly for four seconds—breathing out smoothly, emptying your lungs for four seconds.

- Pause for four seconds—wait four seconds before beginning the next inhalation.

Repeat this exercise for a few minutes a day to start, and then increase both the time and number of times each day as you become more familiar with it and as it becomes more enjoyable.

Strategy #8

Grab a coloring book and some colored pencils.

Coloring books are just for children, right? Wrong!

Creativity of any kind stimulates a different part of the brain than where thoughts are stored. And when that creativity brings us back to our childhood, our mood shifts to pleasant memories that bring us joy. The simple act of coloring is not only creative but also requires concentration—as long as you're the type that stays within the lines.

Coloring books are readily available in retail stores and online and have a variety of themes. The colored pencils allow you to decide what looks best in any part of the picture you're painting (and creating). Sitting down with a coloring book might sound childish, but just 20 minutes at a time (even just once a day) will have you letting go of those old, unwanted thoughts and trading them in for new, healthier ones.

If you're the adventurous (and naughty) type, there are even coloring books filled with swear words. Trust me on this one; it's a great way to let go of what needs to be let go of!

Strategy #9

Listen to calming music.

Every one of us has a list of favorite songs. And when we hear them, they evoke specific memories and emotions. Music can do that, correct?

Some of us listen to a playlist when we're working out, and others when taking a walk or doing another activity. Whatever it is, we have a particular musical taste depending on what we're doing; music helps us with what we're doing.

You can also listen to music with intention. That is, you can listen to specific music to help you let go of thoughts that might be causing you angst or worry. Music known as binaural beats has been used for different effects for decades. To let go of stress and anxiety, it's suggested you listen to binaural beats in the alpha frequency (8-13 Hz). Lower beta frequency binaural beats (14-

30 Hz) have been linked to increased concentration and alertness, problem-solving, and improved memory.

Several online sites (including YouTube) have these for free.

Strategy #10

Change the energy by changing your location.

A dear friend of mine (who died from cancer in 2016) used to tell those attending talks he gave around the country that they needed to change the energy in the room. He would have them get up in the middle of his presentations, walk to the other side of the room, and introduce themselves to those whose seats were there.

The idea was to have those in attendance change the energy they were sitting in and around. By doing so, they had a chance to stretch their legs and feel differently about themselves and people they would not have met if they didn't get up and move.

The same is true for you and me. When we change our physical location (even if it's just a different room in our home), our subconscious minds notice everything different. In doing so, our brains react by determining what information is needed and can be disregarded.

While our brains are busy doing these calculations, our minds shift their focus away from any negative thoughts toward what our unconscious minds tell us is important. We are changing thought patterns by changing our physical location.

So what are you waiting for? Get up and get moving!

Strategy #11

Take a walk.

Everyone knows that exercise is good for us; even moderate movement is good . . . good in a physical way. But what many people don't know are the benefits moderate exercise has on our mental health as well.

Just as most people know that exercise is good, a lot also find it difficult to either get to a gym or commit to a gym membership. There is good news on both the physical and mental side of the exercise benefits deal: It can be both moderate *and* done without the need to get to a gym.

Numerous research studies have demonstrated the benefits of regularly taking a simple 15-20 minute walk. And as stated above, the benefits of taking a walk are physical and mental. For mental health, walking outside is preferred to a treadmill (or laps around the office floor).

When you can get outside, you've already changed your location from where you were having those unwanted thoughts; that's a big advantage that is usually easy to accomplish. When you're walking outside, your mind takes in all the surroundings (sights, sounds, smells, even the way the surface you're walking on feels on your feet). This mental distraction, added to the feel-good hormones released when you walk, gives you the one-two combination that knocks away unwanted thoughts.

Strategy #12

Get some exercise
(*after consulting your doctor).

Ahh, the feel of sweat running into the eyes; it's a great feeling, isn't it?

Okay, maybe a hard, intense workout isn't for everyone, especially for those of us who are disabled or living with chronic pain. But that doesn't mean we can't incorporate some form of exercise into our lives. And the folks who conduct studies on this stuff tell us that just 30 minutes of light to moderate exercise is all that's needed to promote a sense of well-being.

Now, before we go any further, it's important to make this statement: *DO NOT begin any form of exercise without first consulting with your doctor* (the real, medical kind of physician who has the authority to write a medication prescription). That should make my lawyer friends happy.

Exercise releases the feel-good hormones dopamine and endorphins. It also promotes neuroplasticity—the brain's ability to change and adapt as needed. This leads to a growth mindset. A growth mindset is essentially an open mind; a closed mind is the opposite. A closed mind is one that says, "This is the way it's always going to be." A growth mindset asks, "What can I learn from this experience?" and, through neuroplasticity, adapts to new information.

It's easy to imagine the synergistic power of combining a growth mindset with feel-good hormones.

Strategy #13

Question yourself if there is evidence to support your thought.

The ability to ask ourselves tough questions is healthy; being honest with ourselves is a sign of emotional maturity. When we find the strength to ask ourselves and be honest with tough questions, we grow in ways we might not have previously imagined. And that leads to solving problems healthier than if we didn't find that strength.

So, when we ask ourselves if there is evidence to support the thought(s) we have, we can do so with a problem-solving mindset. That allows us also to consider if there are any positives we're ignoring.

You can put yourself in the role of a friend who is having the same thoughts you are. How would you help them problem-solve the issue? What advice would you suggest to them about that thought? How would you gently nudge them to seek out any positives they are overlooking?

Once you have practiced that exercise, ask yourself again what evidence—real evidence (not imagined or feared)—there is to support the way you're thinking. Ask yourself what positives you are either overlooking or ignoring. Finally, give yourself the credit you deserve for having the strength to ask yourself these tough questions.

Strategy #14

Will it matter a year from now?
Five years from now?

Think back to this time last year. What was going on in your life? What was the biggest worry you were experiencing? What about five years ago? What happened five years ago and what was your biggest worry? What was the most significant issue last year this time and five years ago?

When you think about it, there isn't a big percentage of things that go on in our lives (decisions we have to make, problems to be solved, questions we must find answers to) that will matter a year from now. Most of our day consists of different ways of experiencing the same or similar things from all our other days. Only a small fraction of our day is spent making major decisions.

If you agree with the previous statements, you can ask yourself: Will it matter a year from now? Will it matter five years from now?

Strategy #15

Give mindfulness, or another form of meditation, a try.

If you don't think you are one of those people who can completely clear their minds, you're in good company! When I first tried meditation, I thought there was something wrong with me because I could not *not think* about things (remember the white bear?). Only after I learned mindfulness, I understood our minds are literally there to think.

In its simplest form, mindfulness is being aware of the present without assigning any judgment or emotion to it. By experiencing the present moment, using all our senses with a neutral frame of mind, we free ourselves from having to judge it—either as something negative or positive. When mindfulness is practiced regularly, it helps to re-wire the brain to stay in the moment instead of ruminating about the past or fretting about the future.

You can practice mindfulness just about anywhere. Wherever you are right now, stop and become aware of what you are experiencing. Do this without assessing any kind of judgment, whether good or bad. Just be present and take in whatever you are experiencing.

This is the foundation of mindfulness, and if you practice it for a minute at a time, a couple of times a day, you will train your brain to stay in the present instead of thinking about yesterday or worrying about tomorrow.

Strategy #16

Put your thoughts in perspective without judging them.

When we put something into perspective, we give ourselves the opportunity to compare it to something similar. By doing so, we often get a clearer, more objective (and accurate) idea of what we're dealing with.

Once we have this objective and accurate idea of what we're dealing with, we can clarify it and then move on from it. We've seen its importance and significance (or lack of importance and lack of significance), and we're moving on with our lives.

While this strategy is similar to the basic form of mindfulness, it differs in one major way: Mindfulness asks us to take in everything we experience (all of our senses); here, we are focusing exclusively on our thoughts. By seeing them for what they really are and not judging them, we give ourselves an unbiased view of them. The key here is *without judgment*.

When you're having difficult or unwanted (unneeded!) thoughts, set aside a few minutes in a quiet place and put those thoughts in perspective—without judging them. Just see them for what they are. And then feel the freedom that comes when you realize they are just thoughts!

Strategy #17

Remember a time when you moved on without any real damage.

Let's face it (and be honest with each other): None of us have gotten this far in life without a few scrapes and scratches—and we all have the scars to prove it. If you have to, go back and re-read that sentence, and pay particular attention to the part that reads: "Gotten this far in life." We've all gotten this far in life; we're here, we've made it to this day!

No matter the difficulties or issues in our past, we have all made it to this day, and are here despite what we've endured. That means we're, at the very least, strong and resilient. Maybe we're stronger than we give ourselves credit for.

Knowing that you are strong and resilient, think about a memory of a difficult time in your past that caused you to have bad feelings; maybe it was when you were punished as a child (grounded) or when you were dumped for someone else—something like that. Now, remember how you moved on with your life, and no real damage occurred.

If you made it through those times, there's no reason to think you won't make it through this one!

Strategy #18

Cook or bake.

When we get creative, we use parts of our brains that differ from worry and stress. And, when that creativity leads to something we can later enjoy . . . well, that anticipation sets our thoughts on something good in the future.

Cooking or baking not only puts our thinking skills to use but our senses are also heightened because of our expectations for the finished product. In hypnosis, a person's mouth will begin to water, and their cheeks will pucker when given the suggestion they are biting into a fresh lemon. Their brain sends a signal to their mouth that they have just bitten into a tart, juicy lemon.

Your brain is no different when you aren't in a state of hypnosis. Simply imagining what something will smell or taste like will cause some kind of physical reaction. So, go ahead and make your favorite dish or most decadent dessert. The creativity and the anticipation will give your brain a much-needed rest from things you don't need (or want) to think about.

Strategy #19

Re-read your favorite feel-good book.

We all have that one book (or story) that brings back wonderful memories or elicits good feelings. There is a part within each one of us that enjoys a feel-good book, maybe even a specific part of that book. I'll share a favorite book I have, a book that has a feel-good message. The book is *Jonathan Livingston Seagull*. I've read it at least half a dozen times, and I plan on reading it again and again until I get to at least a dozen!

What about you? What book or story do you remember that makes you feel good?

Do you know that when we read something that makes us feel good, our brains release the same feel-good hormones released when we experience something good in person? Just thinking about your favorite book or story now gives your brain a chance to release those hormones.

Reading anything is a good distraction technique. However, there is a lot of material that, when read, can cause us to become anxious or even scared. This is why it's suggested that you re-read a feel-good book or story. By re-reading a book, you already know that it will make you feel good—no surprises. And the anticipation creates a positive distraction where you're free to think about good things.

What are you waiting for? Go grab that book and a cup of your favorite beverage and spend a little time getting lost in the plot.

Strategy #20

Take in a game or show.

J ust as reading a book distracts us from our thoughts, so too can watching a game or a show. Whenever we change our focus, we change our thoughts; and when we focus our attention on something entertaining, we are more likely to become absorbed in it. Whatever we become absorbed in, our thoughts stay in that realm instead of ruminating over worries of yesterday or tomorrow.

Going out to see a show or a sporting event, even (especially!) a local one, will shift our thoughts in several ways. First, we are physically getting away from wherever those unwanted thoughts were holding us hostage. Next, the location where the show or event is taking place will cause our subconscious mind to take it all in and see things we're not used to seeing (the field or court, the stage and the curtains, etc.). Then there's the entertainment value, where we give our brain a reason to express good feelings.

If you can't get out of the house to see a show or a game, try to watch it in a different room in your home from where you normally would take it in. In the same way that the subconscious mind takes in new things at a venue, watching a show or game in a different will cause it to do the same.

The time away (whether physically or emotionally) from your worries will give you a chance to reset things in your mind and come back feeling refreshed and open to feeling the way you want to feel.

Strategy #21

Find those old photos from your past that bring back good memories.

Whether on a smart device or in a scrapbook, old photographs of simpler times are there for the finding. We simply have to set our intention on finding them.

I was recently going through my phone looking for the photo of a serial number from the underside of a water-filtering hookup in our house. It's installed at an angle where you can't see it, so I used my cell phone to take a picture of it. As I went through my photos, I came across one of me with my bomb dog partner—taken 20 years ago. The feelings of seeing that photo brought back are hard to describe.

I'm sure you have a photo on your phone that will bring back good memories. If not on your phone, maybe a scrapbook or an old photo album. Wherever they're located, those old photos are worth finding, and when found, they are certain to give you a reason to smile.

Strategy #22

Practice letting go of what doesn't serve you well.

Practice makes perfect. At least, that's the way the saying goes. And, in this case, you have nothing to lose by giving it a go!

The best way to practice letting go of something is to use a symbolic form of it before you move on to the real thing. It's been said that the worst time to practice something for the first time is when you need it to be right. Who wants to be a medical student's first surgical patient?

It's as easy as taking out the trash to practice letting go of what doesn't serve you well.

The next time you have to take out the trash, look inside the bag before you tie it up. Then, ask yourself if what you see is enjoyable or if it serves you well. This next part might not be easy, but it's important to try: Don't attempt not to notice how it smells. You don't need to stick your nose in the bag and take a deep breath. Just noticing what it smells like is enough to do the trick. Does that smell belong in your home? Does it belong anywhere near you?

When you throw that bag into whatever receptacle is outside, take note of how good it feels to let go of that garbage. You can now use this chore as a metaphor for letting go of what doesn't serve you well.

Strategy #23

Challenge the idea that you have to control everything in order to be content.

One doesn't need to be a control freak to believe they have to control everything to be happy. Many of us don't like the idea of being out of control, and we tend to attach our content-ness to being able to control things. It's as if we believe we'll be happy once we are in control.

This unrealistic idealism creates conflict in all areas of our lives. So the question arises: Do you really need to be in control of everything to be content? When you challenge your previously held beliefs, you give yourself an opportunity to grow.

You can take this opportunity for growth, and in doing so, you'll free yourself from the burden of something unrealistic: that you have the power to control every aspect of your life. If you agree that you have no control over the weather, you can understand how useless it is to try to control things that are out of your control. As the saying and the song goes, "Learn to dance in the rain."

Strategy #24

Write it down and then get rid of it.

One of the most cathartic things we can do is to physically express unproductive thoughts and feelings and then get rid of them. The easiest way to do this is to write them down on a piece of paper.

Wiring down your thoughts isn't anything new, and if you are familiar with journaling, the writing part of this strategy will sound familiar. However, when the thoughts are unproductive, this takes it one step further. After you write down your thoughts, you take that piece of paper and either destroy it or set it free without destroying it.

If you choose to destroy it, you can simply crumple it up and throw it away. If you have access to a firepit or fireplace and are sure it's safe to do so, you can light the paper on fire and watch those thoughts disappear into ash and smoke.

If you'd rather set those free without destroying them, you could imagine tying the piece of paper to a helium balloon and releasing it into the air. Imagine it drifting higher and farther away from you and feel those old feelings weaken until they disappear along with the balloon.

Strategy #25

Talk to a trusted friend or loved one.

Do you remember the game show where you could become a millionaire if you correctly answered a series of questions? If you ran into a problem where you weren't sure of an answer, you could phone a friend. If you watched that show, you know that the contestant chose the friend long before they were actually on the show, and it was a friend the contestant trusted.

We all have that one friend whom we trust, don't we? If not a friend, maybe it's a family member or a coworker. It might even be a counselor or a clergy member.

Talking to someone we trust is a healthy way to let go of unproductive thoughts. Some call this being able to vent.

Venting, or putting our thoughts into words, allows us to release them from our bodies.

Using this strategy relies on trust, and it's essential that you advise the person —at the beginning of the conversation—that you are not asking them to fix anything or give you any advice; you just need them to listen.

Strategy #26

Call a counselor or therapist (or a crisis hotline).

As a former paramedic and retired police detective, I understand the unfortunate stigma of mental health and the reluctance to contact a professional for help. I also understand, from personal experience, the benefits of speaking with a counselor or therapist (I've sat in both types of offices on more than a few occasions).

Counselors and therapists have helped me and some of my family members in ways that would fill another book if I were to list them. Admittedly, the first call wasn't easy, and it took some strength to get past the stigma (and fear) of seeing a professional. But once I made that call, my life changed for the better—almost immediately.

My plea to you, if you're reading this, is to seriously consider this strategy to help you let go of what needs to be let go of.

If you need immediate help, the nationwide crisis hotline number is 988. You can also text "HOME" to 741741.

Strategy #27

Practice positive affirmations.

The late heavyweight boxing champion, Muhammad Ali, is quoted as having said, "If my mind can conceive it, and my heart can believe it, then I can achieve it."

Our subconscious mind constantly listens to our thoughts; some have even called it the constant eavesdropper. Our subconscious mind is like a dutiful servant where it does everything it can to accomplish what it hears. This is why letting go of unproductive and unhealthy thoughts is so important.

It makes sense that if we send positive messages to it, the subconscious mind will also do what it can to see them through. This is where the power of positive suggestions comes into play.

Positive affirmations should be in the present tense and must be *positive* in nature. An example of a positive affirmation is, "I release negative thoughts and feel good about it." Notice it's in the present tense and it is a positive statement. This is *positive* goal-setting. You don't want to get into the habit of negative goal-setting; an example of negative goal-setting sounds like, "I will no longer think negative thoughts." Notice that this statement is something you will not do, not something you will do. Avoid these kinds of affirmations.

A simple and very effective affirmation that has been used for more than 100 years is:

"Every day, in every way, I'm getting better and better."

Strategy #28

Make a mental list of your positive attributes.

Society and most of our family members tell us not to think too much of ourselves; we're conditioned to ignore our strengths and those things others see in us as positive attributes. In that conditioning, we've conditioned ourselves to only hear our faults and shortcomings. Our brains have been trained to ignore (or, at the very least, downplay) our assets and, instead, focus on what's wrong with us.

Some would argue that this is a survival trait that has been in us since we, as humans, began walking on two feet. After all, our ancient ancestors needed to keep refining everything about them to survive.

But we don't live in those times anymore. We don't need to be concerned about outrunning a large mammal that wants to eat us for dinner! But because it's ingrained in our DNA, it's difficult to think positively about ourselves; it's uncomfortable at best.

This is why you must practice it—take time out of your day every day and practice making a list of your assets. Why are you good at something? Why do people enjoy being with you? Why do you enjoy a hobby or activity? Make a mental list of these attributes, and before you know it, your brain will be ignoring the negative self-talk (and thoughts!) and will begin to focus on your strengths.

Strategy #29

Remind yourself that it's okay to not be okay.

I understand an author isn't supposed to have a favorite . . . so I'm not going to say that this strategy is one of my favorites. But I can *think* it, can't I?

Our society strives for perfection, doesn't it? Athletes who perform perfectly, Olympians who get perfect tens, models whose bodies are a ten, restaurant meals and desserts that are perfectly prepared, and students who get perfect grades. All of these, and more, are rewarded by people of all ages. Is it any wonder that people of all ages feel like they've failed if they aren't perfect?

Taking it even a step further, we've been conditioned to believe that we must be at least "okay" in order to succeed in this world.

Yet, we're not always okay, are we? There are times when we're anything but okay. And that's okay!

Reminding yourself that you don't always have to be on, that you don't always have to be winning or succeeding, and reminding yourself that you can be a little (or even a lot) off is a powerful acknowledgment.

It is indeed okay to not be okay, and you can settle in that understanding and take your time as you let go of those old thoughts that had you thinking differently. Reminding yourself that it's okay to not be okay is so powerful that certain authors have been known to write it on their bathroom mirror using a dry-erase marker.

Strategy #30

Recognize what triggers negative thoughts.

Have you ever had poison ivy? I mean, have you ever been affected by the rash and itching resulting from coming in contact with it?

If you've been exposed to it and have suffered that rash, you know how much you try to avoid it when you're outside. You stay away from anything that even looks like it; you want no part in getting close to it. What you are doing is practicing a form of *avoidance therapy*. You're avoiding that very thing that causes you that kind of misery.

Before you practice avoidance therapy, you must first know what causes the discomfort. You know poison ivy causes that itchy rash, so you avoid it.

What causes you uncomfortable or miserable thoughts? By identifying what or who causes them, you can then move on to avoiding them. Here's a key point regarding that: Practice it! The more you practice it, the more natural it will become. And whenever you realize you've avoided a trigger, celebrate it by giving yourself another check in the win column.

Strategy #31

Make a list of your success (wins) for the week.

This strategy has been hinted at in other parts of this book. Most of us don't have experience keeping tabs on our successes—our wins. It's time to change that!

When we change the way we think, we begin to see things differently. And when we see them differently, we experience them differently. This all starts with a mindset that says, "Instead of what didn't go as planned (or hoped), I'm going to start keeping track of my successes this week." In doing this, you're priming yourself to think more positively, which will naturally leave less room for any unwanted thoughts.

Another benefit of this strategy is in the form of the adage, "Success begets success." As you practice keeping track of your wins, you'll notice that you will start to look for them. You'll soon begin to look at problems as opportunities for another win instead of a setback. This shift is known as a growth mindset, and it will be another tool for you to use to let go of those previous crappy thoughts and ideas.

Strategy #32

Step out of your comfort zone and do something different.

The most considerable times of growth come when we are uncomfortable. Well, at least that's what a counselor once told me. But it makes sense, doesn't it? Especially in relationships; relationships grow not when everything is going great. They grow when they are tested. And with growth comes confidence.

When our minds accept discomfort as an opportunity for growth, they more readily accept those situations that aren't favorable to what we had planned for. In doing so, our minds release connections to negative thoughts.

What does it mean to step out of your comfort zone and do something different? Well, if you're a person like me with no singing ability, it might mean singing like no one is listening. And, if you're like me and can't dance to save your life, it might mean dancing like no one is watching. You can try painting or creating other forms of art. You can pick up a musical instrument and give it a try. I know someone who recently began sharing poetry on his social media page. Whatever it is, it will help you grow and that will pay dividends down the road.

Strategy #33

Do random acts of kindness.

Everyone is familiar with the feeling when someone holds the door for us. When it's a stranger, the act sends an unspoken message that regardless of who we are, someone went out of their way (however small) to do something kind for us. Research tells us that we feel this way because of chemicals released in our brains when someone does something kind for us. This research also tells us that those same chemicals are released in the brain of the person doing that act of kindness.

When feel-good chemicals are released in our brains, they help to re-wire our brains where our previous thought pathways are traded for new ones. And those new ones lead to a more optimistic (positive) mindset.

While random acts of kindness release feel-good chemicals and create new thought pathways, when they're done without expecting anything in return, they become a way of life. So when you do random acts of kindness, do them without expecting anything; after all, if you do them expecting something in return, you enter into a contractual interaction instead of pure kindness.

One word of caution: Random acts of kindness can become addictive . . . in a good way!

Strategy #34

Smile.

"If you're happy and you know it, clap your hands!"

C'mon, sing it if you know it!

The byproduct of the joy of watching your twin grandchildren three days a week while Ms. Rachel pays in the background will have you singing it, too. Here's the thing— even if you're not happy, you can still clap your hands until you become happy. The same thing with smiling: You can smile even if you have to force it.

Why?

Because smiling, even if you have to force it, tells your brain that you are happy. Because, since you were a baby, you've been smiling whenever you were happy, your brain associates smiling with being happy. So when you smile when you're not particularly happy, you're tricking your brain into thinking you are.

If you are truly happy, smiling will improve your mood even more. Either way, whether you are happy or not, smiling will make you think differently because your mood will shift.

If you smiled because you sang along with the words at the beginning of this page, give yourself a pat on the pack and remember how that felt; it's that feeling that creates the mind shift you need to let go of unwanted thoughts.

Strategy #35

Change your body position.

Earlier in this book, the strategy of changing your energy was discussed. The working thesis is that when we change the energy around us, we change how we feel. A suggestion in this strategy was to move your physical location to change the energy around you.

In this strategy, we're going to change our body position to change the energy. And the energy we're talking about is the energy within us. This energy shift within us is accomplished because of what our brains have learned from our body position.

Consider our posture when we're sad. What does that look like? Head down, shoulders slumped forward, a sinking stance throughout our torso. Now consider our posture when we're confident. What does that look like? Our head is up, our eyes are focused, our shoulders are back, and our stance is strong.

All of these different body positions (no matter how subtle) give cues to our brains that either direct or reinforce how we are feeling. This means that when you want to release a negative thought, it will be easier and more effective if you change your body position to something other than the way it was when you had that thought.

If your feet are flat on the floor, shift your weight. If you're standing, sit down. And conversely, if you're sitting, stand up. Notice of your body posture and shift it to something different.

Practice this regularly and you'll soon notice how effective it is!

Strategy #36

Commit to making one healthy food choice that day.

What better way to distract you from worry than food, . . . right? If you have a wife like my wife, you would understand that food is the solution to all life's problems.

But you're not married to my wife, so why is this strategy in this book? Great question!

Neuroscientists tell us that good nutrition is good for the brain. And since it's in the brain where thoughts are generated, this sounds like an excellent start to the answer to the question. It's more than just the nutritional importance that makes this strategy work, and it's also training ourselves that when we make a commitment, we'll follow through with it. And finally, the focus of our thoughts changes to something in the future ("I will eat something healthy today."), the present (eating something healthy), and the future ("I will follow through with this and eat something healthy tomorrow.").

The inner dialogue of telling yourself you will do it, then following through with it, reinforces something positive and helps change not only your mood, but your thought pathways.

Strategy #37

Laugh!

D o you remember the movie *Patch Adams*? The doctor, played by the late Robin Williams, believed both the body *and* the soul needed to be treated in order for healing to take place. The movie, based loosely on a true story, demonstrated the power of humor—and laughter—when people are facing difficult times.

As a police chaplain and an ordained minister, I'm often called to be with people dealing with grief. One commonality I've witnessed in all my years doing this work is that healing begins after we give ourselves permission to laugh again. I've seen countless times that people don't need to be happy to laugh.

Keeping your sense of humor, even in times of trouble, can help you more than you might fully understand. Humor helps keep your mind open and is a sign of critical thinking.

This helps you change your thought pattern from something unproductive to something that distracts your mind while causing your brain to release endorphins (feel-good hormones). A win-win scenario if there ever was one!

Here, pull my finger!

Strategy #38

Yell into your head, "Stop!"

If you haven't seen the Mad television skit from 2001, where comedian Bob Newhart plays a psychotherapist, you are really missing something. In the skit, Newhart has a new patient come in for a fear of something. Newhart's solution: "Stop it!" That's it—he tells this new client to "Just stop it!"

We all know life is more complicated than a comedy television show, but that doesn't mean we can't learn something from it. And in this case, there is a kernel of truth in the skit.

This strategy is really a two-part strategy. The first part is to yell, "Stop!" into your head (obviously, you're yelling silently) when you have an unproductive thought. This works by reminding you that you are in control, not that part of your mind that is sometimes referred to as the monkey mind (because it's all over the place with thoughts). The second step is to immediately think about something that brings you pleasure or happiness—maybe a vacation destination, a dear friend or loved one, or a memory of a good time in your childhood.

This one-two combination is effective and can be used whenever you need it without anyone ever knowing what you're doing.

Strategy #39

Practice gratitude.

Similar to doing random acts of kindness, practicing gratitude promotes a positive outlook partly because of the chemicals released by the brain. And just as important is the new way of thinking about life in general. When we practice gratitude regularly, we train our brains to see the world differently—in a more positive (and healthier) way.

When an unwanted thought enters the picture, making a list of three things you are grateful for at that moment will immediately re-direct your focus. The things you are grateful for don't have to be (and probably shouldn't be) anything on a grand scale.

The taste of a morning cup of coffee, the way a new pair of shoes feels, restful sleep the night before, a home-cooked meal, a talk with a friend . . . all of these are just a few examples of simple things to be grateful for in life. Stop taking these life events for granted, identify at least three of them every day, write them down, and then see how your outlook on life changes.

Writing down your gratitude will let you see it in black and white. As you see what you've written, your thoughts will change along with your brain chemistry.

Strategy #40

Set a time limit for any unproductive thoughts.

Although this might sound counterintuitive, acknowledging and staying with unproductive thoughts can be an effective way to let them go . . . as long as you set a time limit and set your intention to move on from those thoughts once the time is up.

Set a timer for anywhere between three and five minutes. Then, sit with those thoughts and just let them do their thing. By practicing this strategy, you don't have to deny them (remember the white bear?). Once the predetermined time is up, congratulate yourself for the courage to be with them, then move on to a productive thought pattern.

An ideal way of accomplishing this is to think of what you want to think about before you begin this strategy. Determine a healthy thought pattern that you want to use before you set the timer. This way, you won't be stuck wondering what to think about when the time expires.

Did you notice, a couple of paragraphs ago, the direction to congratulate yourself? This is just as important as setting the timer and moving on to a productive thought pattern. Positive self-talk doesn't come naturally to most people; practice it now and see how many other aspects of your life change!

Strategy #41

Create a positive and fun anchor.

Pavlov had a dog that salivated at the sound of a bell because the dog had been conditioned to identify the sound of the bell with food. The sound of the bell anchored into the dog's mind the sight, smell, and taste of food. So even if no food was present, the dog still salivated because its brain was conditioned to connect the sound of the bell with food.

Just like Pavolov's dog, we have all been conditioned to associate certain things (like the sound of a bell) with certain activities (like eating food). And many of those conditionings have been *anchored in* by sights, sounds, locations, and physical sensations. We have all heard a song come on the radio, and were instantly transported to a different time, place, and feeling. That song was an anchor.

Now that we know this, we can use it to help us let go of things that don't serve us well.

The simplest way of doing this is to think of something positive—a happy memory, a good mood, a helpful thought. Let that feeling build and as it reaches its peak, take your thumb and forefinger and touch the fingertips as if you're making the "okay" sign. Then squeeze those fingertips together and lock in that feeling—anchor in that sensation.

The next time you have a negative thought hanging around too long, use this anchor to push it away and bring forth a positive one.

Strategy #42

Stop any comparison to others in similar situations.

One of my favorite poems is *Desiderata* by Max Ehrman. A line in it hits home for me: "If you compare yourself with others, you may become vain or bitter, for always there will be greater and lesser persons than yourself."

It's true, isn't it? There will always be greater and lesser persons than ourselves. When we compare ourselves to how others handle situations in their lives, we make a breeding ground for fear, worry, anxiety, and even depression.

Taking cues and learning from others is one thing, but comparing our skills to the skills of others is a recipe for disaster. Instead, we can turn what we witness in others into knowledge and wisdom. Knowledge and wisdom lead to confidence, and confidence takes us to a place of calm and relaxation.

So the next time you feel yourself holding onto an unproductive thought, remind yourself that you have what it takes to deal with whatever the issue is; you can even say to yourself, "All I can do is all I can do. And all I can do is enough."

Strategy #43

Stop "should have" self-talk.

Regrets. I've had a few.

Thank you, Mr. Sinatra.

We've all had them, haven't we? Maybe part of being human is regretting some things we've done (and some of the things we didn't do). But just because it's part of being human, that doesn't mean we have to be prisoners to them. It's important to focus on what we've accomplished (no matter how small it might seem) rather than ruminate over things we wish we would have done.

If you've noticed, the overwhelming majority of the strategies in this book have been positive in nature; that is, they offer suggestions for you to do something (positive goal setting) as opposed to not doing something (negative goal setting). However, the detriment of this kind of harmful self-talk—"I should have done . . ."—is so serious that it deserves this kind of "Stop doing it!" message.

Equally important is after noticing this kind of self-talk (and stopping it), give yourself credit for responding to it quickly. That credit will start a chain reaction of positive self-talk that will serve you well. Because if we let the "would-a, could-a, should-a" talk to continue, we "should-a" all over ourselves!

Strategy #44

Recognize automatic negative thoughts.

Have you ever gotten home from work, shopping, or visiting a friend, and when you pulled into your driveway, you had no recollection of the drive home? Yeah, welcome to the club! It's okay, though; you don't have to worry. You probably drove safer during those times than if you were entirely focused on nothing but driving. That's because you drove in an automatic way while your conscious mind was off doing something else.

This automatic function of our minds is both beneficial and a liability—especially when it comes to thoughts. It is even worse when those thoughts are negative. That's why planning for them and addressing them when they become apparent is important.

While traveling the country teaching school safety and security to law enforcement and school administrators, I told them about my "Six Ps" of an incident. My six Ps of an incident are: <u>P</u>roper <u>P</u>lanning <u>P</u>revents <u>P</u>iss <u>P</u>oor <u>P</u>erformance.

Create a plan now on how you will deal with negative thoughts that seem to come up automatically. Then, implement the plan and congratulate yourself for being proactive!

Strategy #45

Identity what kind of emotions are attached to negative thoughts.

This is a fun strategy because you will come away with a better understanding of how your mind works. It might be a little uncomfortable the first time you use it, but after that, you'll find yourself trying it in many different areas of your life.

The first step is to identify what emotions are attached to your thoughts. For example, ask yourself how it feels (your emotions) when you think about your first teenage crush. Depending on how that worked out, your emotions—your feelings about that—are either good or bad. The next step is to think of something opposite to that experience. If it was a good experience, think of something bad, and if it was a bad experience, think of something good. And notice how your emotions have changed when you changed your thoughts.

Now, identify some negative thoughts you've been having and consider what emotions are attached to those thoughts. Got it? Good!

Finally, change your thoughts to something positive that's happening in your life. And when you do, notice how your emotions have changed as well.

It might sound overly simplistic, but this strategy works. Give it a try!

Strategy #46

Embrace the thought and sit with it for a minute.

"What? Are you crazy, Rusty?"

I hear you. I promise I hear you. Just give me a minute to explain.

You remember the white bear, don't you? Well, I had my own kind of white bear—it was the diagnosis of a tumor growing in my spinal cord. Over the first couple of years, I hated everything about it; I cursed it, and I was angry because of the pain it caused me. And then . . . and then someone suggested that I embrace it for a very brief period and release it by acknowledging the purpose it served in my life. By doing so, I also released all of the anger and resentment.

So go ahead and embrace that negative thought for just a minute, then tell yourself that it served whatever purpose it was meant to serve. And then release it.

By doing this, you are no longer attempting to resist the thought; in a weird way, that thought becomes confused because it's never been treated like this before. And then the power it once had is no longer present—your subconscious mind simply moves on (and away) from it.

Strategy #47

Chunk the problem down to manageable things you can tackle.

E very problem can be compared to a puzzle. There are several pieces to it, and it's all clear when all of the pieces are together.

So many times (I would argue almost all the time), we try to tackle the problem as a whole; we see the picture on the puzzle box and believe that needs to be addressed. Considering some of the puzzles today have thousands of pieces, that can be a daunting task at best.

The good news is that you don't have to attack the problem as a whole. If you step back and see it for what it is, you'll realize that it's almost impossible to do so. So why not break it down piece by piece and work on one of them at a time?

Imagine taking a piece out of a completed puzzle and taking care of that. Then, move on to another piece. And so on and so on.

This is called "chunking it down." Chunking down is used in all areas of life. My wife used to teach it to her high school students before she retired from education.

Chunk down the issue and see how it becomes less intimidating and how more solutions seem to appear.

Strategy #48

Build or create something in your mind.

G rowing up, I had a family member who was a truck driver. Around the time I got my license, I asked him how he stayed awake at night while driving. He told me he built houses in his mind—he built a house from the foundation to the roof in his mind. He said this kept his brain working, and by doing so, it kept him from feeling sleepy.

This kind of distraction works for keeping us from falling prey to unproductive thoughts just as well as it did for my relative, who used it to drive safely through the night. Stimulating the creative part of your brain can have mental health benefits beyond distracting you from your thoughts.

The types of things you can create in your mind are almost limitless. It could be anything related to art (poetry, drawing,

107

painting, sculpting, music), construction (building a house, a shed, a deck, an office building or a warehouse), landscaping (installing a retaining wall, a garden, a driveway, planting shrubbery, designing a new back yard pool area), a craft (ceramics, flower arranging, needlework, wood or leather working, even fashion).

Use your imagination and allow that creative part of your brain to re-focus your thoughts on something creative.

Strategy #49

Go on a virtual shopping spree.

Do you remember when you were a child and would get in trouble for daydreaming during class? No? Just me?

If you were to look around you right now and inventory everything you see, you would be making a list of ideas that came to fruition. Think about that: Everything ever invented or created by humans, was first an idea in someone's mind. These ideas often came about as a result of daydreaming.

You can use daydreaming to your advantage when you want to re-focus your mind. A fun (and cheap!) way of doing this is to go on a virtual shopping spree. You can go on a grocery shopping spree in your mind, visualizing each shelf or aisle. It could be a shopping spree in a home center where you go from department to department and get the best of everything you need for your home. Maybe it's a favorite department store, and you get to select all those things you've always wanted.

Whatever you choose, have fun with it and allow yourself to get as specific as you desire in seeing in your mind every detail wherever you're shopping.

Strategy #50

Enjoy a soothing cup of tea or hot cocoa.

Many practitioners in the medical field have been calling the gut "the second brain." So it makes sense that if we soothe the gut (our stomach), we'll also soothe the brain associated with it.

Notice this strategy is about *soothing* the second brain, not *stimulating* it. When our brains are focused on unproductive thoughts, they are already stimulated. This strategy takes our brains on a 180 turn in the opposite direction to calm and soothe our minds.

The number of calming teas available now seems to be beyond calculation. And while shopping for a calming or soothing tea would certainly help, so would a simple cup of ordinary, regular tea. Sipping it and savoring the warmth calms the mind and can evoke feelings of peacefulness and happiness.

Isn't it easy to recall the happy times of childhood when we would sip a mug of hot cocoa? Those memories are effortlessly recalled just by feeling the warmth of the outside of the mug. That warmth carries in all the sweet chocolate flavor of the drink as we sip it down to our stomach—our gut, the second brain. And that brain responds to the warmth, taste, and memories associated with it to create feelings of serenity and even pleasure.

Strategy #51

Practice reframing the situation.

My wife, Elissa, is a watercolorist. Her paintings are amazing and I'm in awe of her talent. She's created countless paintings and many are hanging in our home; all of them have been framed. She tells me that a frame is almost as important as the painting itself because it sets a tone for the art and makes a difference in how each is seen.

Before I met Elissa, I never gave much thought to a frame around a painting or photo, but now I understand what the purpose of the frame is. Like art, how we frame a situation creates a tone for how we see it. And how we see it dictates how we respond to it . . . even if that response is only our thoughts.

Reframing a situation means seeing it differently; it means taking an old frame off a painting and putting on a new one, creating a new experience of the same thing, By creating that new experience, we see it differently, and we see different things in it differently.

Now that you know what reframing is, you can use this strategy to see problems from a different point of view. You can see them with a new perspective, and by doing so, you can see them differently and see things in them differently.

By reframing situations, you can now reframe your thoughts and how you respond to them.

Strategy #52

Practice self-acceptance.

If you're old enough to remember listening to your favorite songs through the speakers attached to a turntable, you're old enough to remember your favorite vinyl album. If you're not old enough to have ever known the thrill of shopping in a record store at the mall, albums were what many of us craved and talked about in our teenage years.

No matter the album or how much we loved it, there was that one song we weren't thrilled with. But even though it had one clunker of a song, that didn't mean we didn't like the album. In fact, we loved it—we accepted it—even with that song being a part of it. Wouldn't it be nice to accept ourselves—even with our not-so-great songs?

Self-acceptance is about embracing all of our attributes—both the good and the bad. We're accepting everything about ourselves. This is a way of seeing our worthiness without focusing on those we find unacceptable. And if you're a guy like me in your early sixties, gaining too much weight as your hair continues to betray the looks you once had, you begin to understand the importance of self-acceptance!

This might not come easy (at first), and it might feel uncomfortable, but if you persevere and see yourself as that favorite album, any negative self-talk will become a thing of the past.

Strategy #53

Teach something to someone.

Someone much wiser than me once said that a great way to learn something is to teach it. The explanation was that our brain retains information differently when we share it than when we simply try to learn it. When we prepare to teach a topic, instead of trying to just absorb the information, our brains work out what parts have to be shared and in what order.

So when we have thoughts we want to let go of, we can use our brains to decide where and what information to share instead of continuing to absorb more and more information (through more and more thoughts). And it goes beyond that. Think of the information you have about something you know how to do. Now imagine the satisfaction you'd feel by teaching that to someone.

Knowing that you've helped someone learn a new skill or gain additional knowledge about a subject will help boost your sense of self-worth and fill you with gratitude that carries you for a long time.

It's important to state that the skill or knowledge you share doesn't have to be something extraordinary; teaching a child how to read or count can be one of the most rewarding things you'll do all day.

Strategy #54

Tell someone why you appreciate them.

In 2021, I published a unique type of gratitude journal. It was a journal not just about gratitude. It was about *sharing* gratitude. The name of it is *The Living Eulogy Journal*, and it offers the user a year's worth of weekly opportunities to tell people in their life they are appreciated. The idea came to me after I officiated a memorial service and witnessed people share their memories of the deceased with his family and friends who were gathered. *Why is it,* I thought, *that we wait until someone is dead before we share our memories about them?* Hence the title of the journal, *The Living Eulogy Journal*.

The emotions a person feels when they share their appreciation for another are special and unique. But a common theme is gratitude; when we share gratitude (not just feel it), our mindsets shift dramatically. Along with that shift is a transformation of our moods . . . and our thoughts. Our entire ways of thinking change.

It might seem uncomfortable at first, but once started, sharing gratitude with others by telling them how much you appreciate them will become a habit you'll never want to break!

And, as has been mentioned in other strategies in this book, when our thinking shifts to something positive, we let go of those old thoughts that don't serve us.

Strategy #55

What advice would you give a friend if they were having the same thoughts?

Me? Give advice? Who am I to give advice to someone who is struggling with stinkin' thinkin'? Yep, that's a term I use for negative self-talk—for thoughts that don't serve us well.

All of us—every one of us—have a lot of experience in stinkin' thinkin'; we've had a lifetime to perfect it and to witness it when it's shared by people around us. And I bet there's not one of us who hasn't shared some advice with a friend, a loved one, a colleague, or a neighbor whose thinkin' was stinkin'.

So now it's your turn to once again share some of the advice you've given others who were struggling with unproductive thoughts. And you can have some fun with this as you activate a different part of your brain to find solutions to a problem.

Instead of standing in front of a mirror and talking to yourself, create an avatar in your mind. Imagine another you standing (or sitting) over there—someplace near you. This person has just confided in you what they are feeling; they've shared the thoughts they want to release so they can move forward in the days ahead.

What advice would you give them?

Listen to yourself and know that you have inside of you all you need to let go of those thoughts inside of you!

Strategy #56

Convert your inner critic into your inner cheerleader.

Maybe you've heard of the term, "inner critic." It refers to the inner voice we have, a voice that is exponentially more negative than positive. It's that voice that is constantly critiquing what we do. It's the words we use to beat ourselves up with, and it's the sound of criticizing our actions and intentions. It creates fear and anxiety. It whispers, "You shouldn't be doing this," or, "You can't do this," or, "Something bad is going to happen if you . . ."

As mentioned in another part of this book, this inner dialogue can be described as "stinkin' thinkin'."

Those in the world of psychology tell us the inner critic is normal and has been in humans since we learned how to walk on two feet. It's kept us alive when survival was paramount in our existence. Times have changed since humans' first attempt at starting a fire, and maybe it's time to change the inner critic into something more useful for us in the 21st century.

Maybe the time has come to turn your inner critic into your inner cheerleader!

As the adage goes, "Practice makes perfect." So, instead of trying to quash your inner critic (recall the problem trying to suppress the white bear), you can convert it into a cheerleader of sorts that encourages you instead of criticizing your every attempt to enjoy life.

Start small. Make a conscious effort to talk to yourself (in your head) in a positive way about something. You can even use a past success (a win) to congratulate yourself and then take that a step further to encourage yourself about a minor task that needs to be completed. Then, use that to build a foundation of positive self-talk: your new inner cheerleader.

Strategy #57

Accept your shortcomings.

The psychologist Michael Yapko, in a peer-reviewed journal, wrote, "What you focus on, you amplify."

That makes sense, doesn't it? When we focus on something, it becomes bigger (and more important) in our minds. So, if we focus on our shortcomings, they will *amplify* in our minds.

What if we were to accept them and see them as just one of our traits, and then move on with other—more important—things in our lives? What would our lives look like if we accepted our shortcomings instead of beating ourselves up over them?

One of my shortcomings is not planning ahead. I'm more of a *fly-by-the-seat-of-my-pants* kind of guy. While serving the church, I never gave a sermon from behind the pulpit. I just talked with the congregation from an open stair in front of the altar. There was no script, no written sermon . . . just a few notes scribbled down.

You can imagine my panic when I neglected to ensure the bread was there for communion one Sunday morning. The only store open at 7 a.m. on a Sunday morning was a local convenience store. All they had in the bread category were Thomas' English Muffins. Imagine explaining that one to the congregation!

But here's the thing: Instead of beating myself up over this misstep, I accepted it as part of who I am and used it as a learning experience. As the cartoon character Pop Eye used to say, "I yam who I yam and that's all what I yam."

Practice it, and it becomes more natural and even more enjoyable!

Strategy #58

Stop second-guessing yourself.

Here is another strategy on how to stop doing something. It sounds simple, but to make it work, there has to be something to replace it with. Nature doesn't like a vacuum—it will fill that void with something. So why not make it something positive?

The first step in this strategy is to imagine a glass in front of you is filled with a liquid that is not good for you—in this case, it's second-guessing yourself. You want to fill the glass with something healthy, something that is beneficial and promotes confidence. But since the glass is full, you can't add any of this to it. So, the first step has to be emptying the glass of the negative stuff.

Self-confidence is different from arrogance. Being trained in a seminary that a Benedictine brother founded, I found it hard to work on my confidence because it felt like I was being arrogant. Dump out of your mind the notion that self-confidence makes you arrogant, and you'll be on your way to being comfortable with the decisions you make and the freedom that comes when you leave them behind.

Now, you can fill that glass with the truth that is yours—that you are okay with being who you are and with your decisions. In doing so, that metaphoric glass becomes a vessel from which you can taste both confidence and freedom.

Strategy #59

Think about what's possible.

So many times in life, we fall into the trap of thinking in absolutes—thinking in black or white. This is usually a trap we set for ourselves because we exclude all other possibilities— the gray area of life.

A dear friend who died from cancer some years ago was a nationally known motivational speaker and best-selling author. He shared his wisdom freely, and one of the wisest things he shared with me was to think of outcomes in the realm of possibilities, not expectations.

He reasoned that expectations have limits—they are capped at a certain point, And we either reach that expectation, or we don't. This can lead to disappointment when we don't reach them, and even when they are attained; once they're reached, we often feel like, "What now? Is this all there is?"

Possibilities are different because possibilities are endless. Possibilities give us options and are flexible and dynamic (an expectation is static and inflexible).

So the next time you're faced with an issue, instead of setting an expectation on how you think it should be resolved, think of all the possibilities and then plan how you'll approach them. In doing so, you'll approach life's challenges with a different, more flexible mindset.

Strategy #60

The worst possible thing isn't going to happen!

In both of my careers as a paramedic and a police officer, I was trained to "Plan for the worst, but hope for the best."

This type of training became a habit of mind—a mindset. It was a mindset that I thought was a great way of thinking because I would always be ready and could be counted on as a person who could handle anything. Unfortunately, this led to me catastrophizing every situation in my life.

In looking back at that time frame (the 30 or so years I spent in the field of emergency services), I see just how unhealthy this was. I also realized that I was not alone in this mindset; one doesn't have to work in the field of emergency services to fall into the trap of thinking the worst will happen.

We all know at least one person who does this, right? They immediately go to the worst possible scenario and then act as if it's already taken place. They're a mess in their emotions; no matter what we say, it doesn't get through to them. Well, thank God that person isn't you or me!

Yeah, right.

Here's the thing: It's normal to prepare for the worst-case scenario; it's something that's in all our DNA for survival. But that doesn't mean you're stuck with it. You can look at the facts, ask for a trusted opinion, and then think about other possibilities instead of dreading the future.

Strategy #61

Develop an attitude of gratitude.

The benefits of gratitude have been discussed in other strategies. This strategy, however, is specific to a grateful mindset. Think of the strategy of practicing gratitude as a cousin to this strategy.

When we practice gratitude, our brains secrete chemicals that make us feel good. This often leads to gratitude becoming a habit. And that habit can soon become an attitude. In one of his popular songs, the singer-songwriter, Jimmy Buffett suggests that we change our attitude by changing our latitude. In this case, I must beg to differ with the man who once had us all looking for our lost salt shaker.

Developing a new attitude takes practice *and* commitment. Setting the intention to do both so we see the world through a lens of gratitude is a gift of opportunity, unlike most other gifts we can give ourselves.

I believe you are worthy and deserving of such a gift!

Strategy #62

Create new neuropathways by creating new habits.

"If you always do what you've always done,
you'll always get what you've always got."
~ Henry Ford

If Mr. Ford was correct, it means if we want to change how things are going for us, we have to change how we manage them. To do that, we must be willing to change. I would suggest that if you are reading this, you have already decided that you are willing to make some changes in your life.

Creating new habits—new healthy habits—is a fun and effective way to create new pathways for thoughts to travel. The folks who get paid lots of money to research this kind of stuff call these neuropathways. When new neuropathways are created, the old (unproductive) ones fade away. Once the brain becomes accustomed to this new way of thinking, this thinking becomes the most direct route of one thought being connected to another.

Can you think of any better way to create new thought pathways than by creating new, healthy, and fun habits? I can't!

Strategy #63

Limit editorial news and media.

Years ago, I promised myself that I would do everything in my power to avoid publishing political statements (whether in published print form or on social media sites). And I'm going to keep that promise with this strategy.

Regardless of what side of the political aisle you side with, editorial news shows—those found on cable channels—are produced to make the owners of those stations money. Period. End of story. Revenue for these media outlets is generated from advertising. Advertisers pay a fee based on ratings—the higher the ratings, the more the stations can charge.

These stations have learned that nothing creates high ratings more than fear and controversy. If they can instill fear in their viewers, they know those viewers will watch their shows for longer periods. Based on numerous studies backed up by decades of research, they know that fear is the best way to keep viewers tuned to their channel.

Fear is necessary for our survival, but it can also be detrimental to our well-being.

One of the reasons, perhaps the biggest reason, we hold on to negative, unproductive thoughts is our fears. If so, why add more of it to our lives?

Stepping away from political discourse and the media outlets (including blogs and social media) that spew fear-mongering is one of the healthiest ways to begin a new mindset that promotes peace, happiness, and gratitude.

Strategy #64

Create a safe place in your mind.

When we were children, we were encouraged to use our imaginations. Then, as we got older, we were told to stick to reality. And now, as grown adults, we rarely use it at all—at least in a healthy, productive way.

This is your chance to relive your childhood in a very real way: It's time to use that imagination of yours again.

Think of a time in your life when you were happy and content. It could be any place you like—a vacation spot, a place outdoors, a room in your home, or a time with a friend or loved one. Any place you remember being happy and content is what it's supposed to be.

Now, take a minute or two and recall everything about that place: the sights and sounds, the way it felt, even any aromas or tastes associated with it. When you have that feeling going really strong, bring yourself back to reality.

Throughout the days and weeks ahead, take this virtual trip back to this place, and while you're there, work on whatever needs to be worked on—especially releasing negative thoughts.

Strategy #65

You're not a mind-reader.

"I know why she's mad at me."

"He said that because he doesn't like that other guy."

"You knew why I asked you to do it."

So many times, we believe we know what someone is thinking; we claim to know their motives and even their beliefs. And we often expect those closest to us to know what we're thinking.

Of all the traps we set for ourselves, perhaps the most troublesome is when we practice mind-reading (or assume others can read our minds). It can, and often does, cause us more trouble in relationships than other communication issues.

When we think we know what another person is thinking, we tend to dream up worst-case scenarios, and then they become real in our minds. Is it any wonder we can't let go of some of our unproductive thinking?

As much as we might know someone, there is no way of stating with certainty that we know exactly what they're thinking. And conversely, as deeply as someone knows us, they can't possibly know exactly what we're thinking. So, we need to stop this mind-reading trap for both ourselves and those we care about.

When it comes to those thoughts that don't serve you well, letting go of the notion that you know what's in the mind of someone is a great first step in releasing them. It will probably feel like you just let go of 100 pounds of useless crap!

It's Time to Let Go

(And say goodbye to the white bear)

While serving at the seminary working with chaplain students, I got to know many wonderful people. And one student of mine stands out whenever I recall those memories. His name was Flying Hawk, and he was a Native American living on a reservation in the Great Plains region of the United States. This is the reservation where the poorest of Native Americans live.

Flying Hawk was his given Native American name, and he was as wise as he was kind. He taught me more about life than I could have ever taught him about chaplaincy work. One of the lessons Flying Hawk taught me was the changing of the color of leaves and the reason they fall to the ground every autumn.

His culture believes the leaves represent the memories of each tree. They hold the memories of the animals playing on the branches, the birds looking for food, baby birds being born, and even of the tree itself—the 360-degree view each tree has of its surroundings.

The leaves change colors to remind the tree of all it has witnessed over the past year, a reminder that soon the leaves will fall off. The leaves must fall off for new memories to be created the following year, and the reason the leaves don't fall off all at once is that the tree needs to hold onto some memories longer than others.

Once all the leaves have fallen to the ground, there's a ceremonial burning of them. All the leaves are gathered into a pile, and everyone comes out to witness this sort of bonfire. There is meditation and prayer to the Great Spirit, and the leaves are set on fire. In doing so, any hurt connected to the leaves is released to the Great Spirit. Any pain, suffering, or hurt attached to memories of those in attendance is released to the sky. That way, new memories can be created in the hearts of the people of that reservation.

What if we took the lesson Flying Hawk shared with me, and instead of memories, we saw leaves in the trees as thoughts? Think of the times we felt compelled to hold on to unproductive thoughts and the times we refused to release the pain associated with some of our thoughts. Why was it so hard to let go of sh!tty thoughts?

Our brains have a limited capacity for thoughts. Why would we want to hold onto anything that prevents us from having positive, happy thoughts? Why would we allow opportunities for gratitude to be pushed aside because our minds are filled with memories of crap we no longer need?

144

Now when we see a tree, maybe it can remind us of how far we've come. Maybe when we see a tree, it can be an anchor to bring up and recall the strategies we've used to let go of thoughts we no longer need. And maybe, now, when we see a tree, we'll feel empowered to take the action needed to be the best version of ourselves.

Goals and Objectives

In a couple of the strategies in this book, I shared that my wife, Elissa, is a retired high school teacher. In that role for more than 37 years, she taught business courses to the students, and for the last 15 years of her tenure, she led a graduate course to new teachers as a requirement for tenure in the school district.

When Elissa taught the teachers, one of the topics was how teachers need to create goals and objectives—specifically, how teachers should identify an attainable goal for each lesson plan they prepare and then specify objectives for students to reach that goal. One of the things I recall about her preparing to teach that block of instruction was her stating the goals and objectives should be presented by the teacher at the beginning of each class. That way, the students in the class clearly understood what was expected of them.

So, of course, it makes sense for me, Elissa's husband—the guy who heard her prepare for her classes countless times—to put the goals for this book at the end instead of the beginning. I can't wait for her to read this. Oh, the answers I'm going to have to come up with when I'm asked why I put the goals for this book at the end of it!

If you give me a few seconds, I think I can explain it (even to Elissa).

If you recall a couple of paragraphs ago (the last sentence to be exact), teachers share their goal for a lesson with their students so they "clearly understand what's expected."

Maybe you can remember one of the strategies where I compared expectations to possibilities. Expectations have limits, while possibilities are limitless. When you started this book, would you have rather felt that the benefits of the strategies presented in it had limits or that they were limitless?

Now that you've finished the strategies part of the book, you can create your own goals on how you will use them in your life. And those goals deserve to be limitless. If you want to take this a step further, consider creating intentions rather than goals. Intentions are flexible and dynamic. They can change with the situation. Set your intentions and then create a plan to reach them.

We've established the purpose of goals and objectives and compared goals to intentions, so let me share my intentions for writing this book. By that, I mean, what did I hope you, the reader, would get out of it when you finished it. What were my intentions for you? What were my hopes in writing this book for someone who wants to release unproductive thoughts?

My first intention in writing this book, my hope, is that anyone who picks it up and reads it will come away with an understanding that the thoughts they've been having—those old, unproductive thoughts—are completely normal. They are *so normal* that we all have them; everyone has had those thoughts and continues to have them. Knowing that the way you've been thinking is completely normal, and knowing that you are in good company in struggling with that type of thinking, hopefully encourages you to see yourself in a healthy way. If you are encouraged to see yourself in a healthy way, you just might be empowered to take action.

My second intention in writing this book is to empower the reader to take whatever action is needed to let go of toxic thoughts and change negative self-talk into something positive. When people are empowered, they tend to see things through instead of allowing things to go unfinished. When you feel empowered to take action, you begin to make changes that benefit you and everyone concerned with your life. Those changes you are making build a foundation where you can create the life you want—the life you deserve. In creating this life, you are becoming the best version of yourself.

My third intention, my undying hope, is that you will feel empowered to believe that you are worthy and deserving of being the best version of yourself.

Knowing that you are as normal as the next person and feeling empowered to make whatever changes are needed, you can see that you are worthy and deserving of being the best version of yourself. I'm not talking to some other person who picked up this book; I am telling *you* that *you* are worthy and deserving of being the best version of yourself!

You are worthy and deserving because there are no limits to what you can become or the possibilities of what you can accomplish. Whatever intentions you set for yourself, remember that you now have the tools necessary to create the life you deserve.

You have renewed strength to let go of old habits and create new ways of thinking; you have the knowledge necessary to make sound decisions based on the facts, not your emotions, and you see things from a different perspective so you have the knowing belief in yourself to problem-solve life's challenges.

These are my intentions for this book; these are my hopes. And I hope you (and Elissa!) now understand why I put them here instead of at the beginning of the book.

One Last Metaphor

Best-selling author Michael A. "Mickey" Singer uses a metaphor for letting go. He describes the benefits of letting go in order to be more fully present. He asks his readers to imagine a stream with a lot of rocks in it. These rocks create disturbances in the flow of the stream and prevent the stream from flowing calmly and freely. In his metaphor, we can use the rocks as our unwanted thoughts—the thoughts we need to let go of.

These rocks that block the free flow of water are the thoughts that are constipating our brains—the things creating cranial constipation. The stream actually starts to back up if there are too many rocks in the path of the flowing water… just like sh!tty thoughts that cause our brains to back up and become clogged.

The key to living our best life, to becoming the best versions of ourselves, is to remove the rocks from our "stream." When we imagine this stream, Singer says a person's natural inclination is to remove the rocks and throw them out of the stream. However, that can't happen because we are the ones holding them in place. We can't toss aside something that we are holding down. We first have to commit to letting go of our hold of it.

When we let go of the rock, it naturally loosens and will float away on its own. Knowing this, we can take our time and let go of each rock, one at a time, and enjoy the feeling we get from watching them naturally float away down the stream. Really get that picture in your imagination: In your mind's eye, imagine letting go of the rocks and what they look like drifting away, floating down the stream. Now notice (again, in your mind) how freely the stream is flowing. Really get into this and allow yourself the time needed to fully embrace this image into your memory.

As the stream now flows smoothly, calmly, and even peacefully, so too can your thoughts and the pathways created with this new mindset. The blockages—the crap that was causing your brain to be constipated—are now gone, and things are flowing as they should. You did it, and you should be proud of the work you've put in. It was certainly better than enduring an enema, wasn't it?

You can now congratulate yourself. Seriously, take a moment and feel good about yourself!

(You feel lighter already, don't you?!)

Other Books by the Author

Finding Gratitude in H.O.P.E.: How Humor, Optimism, Patience, and Empathy Can Help Us Accept What We Find Unacceptable

"A must-read book for anyone searching for hope."

G-Pa Has Stinky Feet

"A delightful children's book."

What We Learned From Fostering Dogs: One Family's Journal of Pee, Poop, Heartache, and Unconditional Love

"I laughed, I cried, I rejoiced!"

Tender Truths: Caring For the Dying (contributing chapter author)

"A treasure trove of practical information for those facing another's death."

The Living Eulogy Journal: A Year of Sharing Gratitude and Becoming Happier

"This book changes the very paradigm for embracing gratitude as a daily practice."

Doubt On Trial: An Agnostic Minister's Case For Questioning The Bible

"Doubt On Trial is a must-read!"

Doubt On Trial: Jury Notes – Journaling Your Thoughts During Doubt's Testimony

"Thought-provoking, interesting perspective on reading the Bible."

About the Author

The author (that would be me) would like to take this opportunity to thank you. Thank you for allowing me to share a little bit of my life with you. Thank you for taking time from your busy life to spend it with me (well, at least with my thoughts). And thank you for reminding me that my life has value. You see, by writing this book, I have learned some things about myself and I believe what I had to say might benefit at least one person. What a gift you have given me!

Everything you need (or would want) to know about me is in the book. However, I'd love to connect on social media; you can find me on Facebook, Instagram, and LinkedIn. If you'd like to see what's going on in my daily life, I post regularly on Facebook and offer weekly sermonettes on Sundays. Find me there as *Rusty Williams, Author.*

And I'd love to hear from you if you have any suggestions or comments about the book. If you'd like to contact me, visit www.TheBarefootMinistries.org

Made in the USA
Middletown, DE
10 October 2023

40367388R00102